GOLEMS

GOLEMS

Poems by

Tina Hacker

Cover design by Shay Culligan

Cover Illustration by Terry Lee

ISBN: 978-1-954353-63-3

Kelsay Books
502 South 1040 East, A-119
American Fork, Utah, 84003

To Lynn,
My loving husband and most enthusiastic fan.
To Alarie and Teresa,
Poetry sisters who helped conjure the golems with me.

Acknowledgments

With special thanks to the online journal *Quantum Fairy Tales* for serializing my golem poems, publishing 14 before the site retired.

"Golem Gets Tattooed" Issue 5, fall 2013
"A Golem in Wonderland" Issue 6, winter 2014
"A Rose Is a Rose" Issue 7, spring 2014
"Disgrace the Demon" Issue 8, summer 2014
"Golem Tastes Chocolate" Issue 9, fall 2014
"Enough Is Enough" Issue 11, spring 2015
"Golem Takes a Cruise" Issue 12, summer 2015
"Shakespeare's Editor" Issue 13, fall 2015
"The Wedding Guest" Issue 15, spring 2016
"Golem Laughs" Issue 16, summer 2016
"A Golem Returns Memories" Issue 17, fall 2016
"The Motorist" Issue 18, winter 2017
"An Angel Flowers" Issue 19, spring/summer 2017

Poetry Super Highway, Holocaust issue, April 2018: "A Golem Returns Memories," Holocaust issue, April 2021: "A Golem Delivers"

Some of these poems have been slightly revised.

Contents

His mourning cries reached deep into the earth and created a golem.

What Is a Golem?

According to several ancient sources, Adam may have been the very first golem!

Arising from Jewish folklore, a golem is a mud and clay being summoned from the earth to accomplish a task dictated by its creator. After fulfilling the task, the golem returns to the earth, becoming mud and dirt again.

The creature is famous for being heroic, like the golem of Prague who saved the Jewish community in the 16th century. But through the ages, the concept of the golem has evolved. Sometimes a golem looks exactly like a human. At other times, it may be a giant or have an ungainly, grimy shape. A golem can be male or female, sexy, funny, or mischievous. It can change its shape as needed, travel back in history, and perform magical and mystical deeds.

I was intrigued by the golem in *The Puttermesser Papers* by Cynthia Ozick. Here was a golem who was female, sassy, and didn't resemble any golem I had encountered in stories or poetry. On a whim, I wrote a couple of poems that put golems in contemporary settings. Golems seemed to circle me day and night until I had a collection.

The golems are helpers in my poems. Some have names; others are satisfied with the name, "Golem." In each piece, the golem receives a task; at the end, it disappears often into the earth as tradition suggests. Though a few of these golems may escape to places only the reader can find.

I'm convinced a golem summoned me.

I am a GOLEM.

Get a wish for FREE!

Enough Is Enough

Task: Come clean about being a golem.

"I exist and the world should know it,"
Golem proclaimed.
The woman who brought him to life agreed.
Golem stood on a street corner
holding a sign. "Will help you for free."
Before long a car came by
but the driver yelled, "Get a job!"
A five-year-old threw gnawed
chicken wings at his head.
A teen shoved a flyer into his hand.
"Lose Fifty Pounds or Your Money Back."
Then rushed away,
drenching her hands in Purell.

Frustrated, Golem raced
to the nearest Walmart and landed
a job as a greeter. Soon every
greeter wore a sign like his.
"Will help you for free."
Customers didn't look at him
or at any of the others.
No one realized a miraculous being
stood in the entrance.
Golem decided he wasn't
imposing enough. He grew as large
as an SUV, turned his eyes
into glowing green orbs, changed his sign.

"I am a GOLEM. Get a wish for FREE!"

Crowds photographed him
with their iPhones, friended him
on Facebook, texted about him on Twitter
before he vanished.

An Angel Flowers

Task: Fulfill a child's wish.

Abbey needed help.
Her nightly dreams about angels
convinced her one could make her well.
Maybe forever, maybe for just a while.

She shouted at the springtime sky,
hoped an angel would hear.
Instead she conjured a golem.
He couldn't cure Abbey
so he decided to bring her an angel.

The golem created a kaleidoscope
of flowers in a park where the child often rested.
He persuaded the wind to twirl,
bend, loop, weave through the blooms,
freeing petals to play in the air, form shapes.

Apple blossoms fabricated fluttering wings.
Crocus and Hyacinth formed
a diaphanous robe that danced
around a lithe body of stems and leaves.
A rainbow of Tulips molded a face
with a mesmerizing smile, tender eyes.

The golem's angel found Abbey
sitting on a bench and enveloped
the little girl in her velvety wings,
healing, consoling, loving her.

As he sank into the arms of soil nearby,
the golem knew Abbey's memories
of this angel would be a balm,
ease symptoms, effects, treatments.
Maybe forever, maybe for just a while.

Golem Gets Tattooed

Task: Find the coolest design.

Golem studied books of flowers,
dragons, stars, wings, naked
dancers, Superman, Batman, Spider
Man, rejected Walmart, Starbucks,
Hello Kitty logos.

Bypassing piercing, punching,
pricking, scratching, he settled
for a modern tattoo gun
and "Sue Stinga," a smokin' ink
maven from Chicago's south side.

Then he selected calligraphy.
"Golem, Golem, Golem"
repeated in exotic
fonts on his arms, legs, forehead
and one butt cheek.

Positive his solution belonged
in the annals of tat couture,
Golem injected his inked body
into the grounds of the Smithsonian.

A Golem Returns Memories

Task: Comfort a Holocaust survivor.

Ruth, the lucky one,
traveled to New York with her aunt
before Hitler's henchmen
brought urban renewal to her town.
She lost parents, cousins,
brother Sam. A sister, unnamed,
still in her mother's womb.

At night she sang Yiddish lullabies
remembered from her childhood
to children she never had.
Didn't know all the lyrics so made some up,
unaware that her words conjured a golem
beneath her window.

Sitting on a lawn chair, the golem
listened to her weeping,
discovered she had only three photos
left of her family. She mourned
lost images that would
stop the slow fading of memories.

The golem explored antique stores
for old photos and frames.
Then changed hairstyles, dresses,
heights, expressions
to reflect Ruth's features
and those of her relatives.

He bought a ragged fan, an ashtray,
a cracked teacup she might find familiar.
When her doorbell rang, the mail carrier
handed her a package from Europe.
A note inside told her the contents
came from her parents' home.

The writer apologized
for keeping her photos, mementoes
so many years before returning them.
The postage marks, signature
were mud-smudged, illegible.
No return address.

Decision Day

Task: Protect and encourage.

"I can vote!" Ruth thought
on the morning of her 18th birthday.
Demanding attention, voices of ABC, CBS, CNN
anchors announced the countdown
to Election Day. A confetti drop of political signs
blanketed her neighborhood.

Ruth felt excited; she could finally
march in this loud parade of feuding choices.
But she also heard the polls might
not be safe; someone might threaten her.
Yearning to vote in person warred with fear
until a golem arose from Ruth's web of thoughts.

"Trust me," he said.

As Ruth stood in line to vote, her faith
in the golem was tested. Nearly blocking
a path to the entrance, a group of men glared
at the voters. Ruth cringed; the woman
standing in front of her whimpered; a man
behind her hunched over, trying to look smaller.

Then the golem arrived.
His demeanor left no question about who was in charge.

When he approached the menacing group,
they backed away though the sign he held
promoted a contender they hated. Ruth stopped
being afraid; everyone stopped being afraid.

Each person in line saw their chosen candidate's
name on the golem's sign.

After casting her ballot,
Ruth searched for her protector.
He was nowhere to be seen
but the sun glinted off
an "I Voted" sticker lying on the grass nearby.

Golem Takes a Cruise

Task: Evaluate the cruising experience.

Golem wore diamonds, silk and Chanel
to the Grand Dining Room
and left generous tips,
so her personal waiter and sommelier
hovered over her each night.
At the all-you-can-eat buffet,
no one complained
when she put 20 pieces
of lox on her bagel.
And ate 12 bagels.

After a few martinis,
she braved the swimming pool.
Her swan dive drew applause
from other tourists as she rose
in triumph from the now muddy water.
She didn't care
that she was missing a toe.

She liked the casino best.
Despite blotchy fingerprints
on dice and cards, Golem was popular.
Her bets complemented
her size that grew bigger every day.
She never turned in a critique
of the cruise. Rumor has it
that she won a million dollars
and is sunning in Fiji.

Disgrace the Demon

Task: Make Hitler a laughingstock.

Spotlights turned night into day on the Zeppelinfeld—Hitler's fairground—when evening parades awed thousands. Nearby, inside a building bearing the omnipresent Reich Eagle and swastika, generators spat electricity at the spectacles.

Unlike other wartime buildings, this one is not a ruin. It still stands, visible to passersby. Golem could destroy it, but ridiculing Hitler was more delicious.

Golem tried to conjure a symbol of American life, something that would rankle Hitler's ashes. Nothing political or obvious. He rejected flags, statues, autos, Oscars and the Constitution. Then the perfect icon appeared: the hamburger.

The competition began: offerings under yellow arches, meat squares from Wendy's, burgers smashed, broiled, made of turkey, chicken and soy.

But the Whopper—the giant among burgers—won. A Burger King opened in the generator building in July, 2006.*

Golem, the first customer, visited only once. He admired the bright neon sign not far from the shadow on the wall left by the Reich Eagle. Chortling between bites, he downed several dozen Whoppers. The servers were glad he didn't visit a second time.

Such a mess to clean. And that strange laughter.

*Actual event.

On the March

Task: Support the Black Lives Matter protest.

Thousands strong, the crowd
was so focused on their shared purpose
that not one person noticed the golem
rising from the shoulder of the road.

And he was very noticeable.
Nearly seven feet tall, the golem had a physique
that would make Mr. Universe envious.
His bulging biceps and toned abs
didn't impress the other marchers at first.

They exuded their own power.
Their commitment to justice rivaled the strength
of the unknown stranger among them. Believing
his task was already fulfilled, the golem turned
to depart when he sensed a darker intent,

saw a handful of people running toward
a popular coffee shop, ablaze with desire
to destroy, loot, create chaos.
In an instant, he stood in front of the store,
ready to thwart the attack.

Protestors and onlookers gaped
when the golem caught projectiles mid-air.
They flinched when fire fizzled in his huge hands.
Cheered as he seized, then destroyed weapons.
The struggle didn't last long.

A little girl shouted, "That big guy was Mexican.
Like me. He spoke Spanish with my accent."

A man nearby corrected her. "It's obvious he's Black. Looked like Jay Z. Didn't you see his BLM tee-shirt?"

A teen standing behind him confided, "I've seen him somewhere. He's Jewish. He wore a *yarmulke* and a silver Star of David!"

"That wasn't a star. It was a cross," an older woman insisted, "a large cross."

The golem was last seen taking a knee on the ballfield in a nearby park.

Escape Now

Task: Liberate a neighbor.

Abe and Heinrich,
friends close as cobbles on the streets
of their town in Germany.

When turmoil seethed around them,
some people blamed England and France.
Some blamed the United States.
Most blamed Jews.
Six months before *Kristallnacht,*
Heinrich told Abe it was time
to emigrate, his voice breaking
like a violin string. Abe wouldn't listen.
He owned a successful shoe factory,
had good friends, a life as smooth as Brie.

Remembering Abe's attempts to conjure
a golem when they were children,
Heinrich summoned one of his own.
He ordered him to convince Abe to escape.
With the tenacity of the burgeoning SS,
the golem summoned bad luck.
Abe's factory equipment rusted overnight,
desire for his shoes dwindled,
neighbors snubbed him in the park.

Confused, frightened, Abe heard
Heinrich's warnings in his dreams,
unremitting fugues amplified
by the golem's powers.

Believing he would soon go mad,
Abe gathered his family and left Europe
a week before a mob burned his factory.
The golem vanished among the ashes
as Heinrich watched the fire
and the Brown Shirts watched Heinrich.

The Newest Friend

Task: Cure Covid-19 loneliness.

"Taking out the trash has become an event,"
Esther thought as she carried two bags of garbage
to the dumpster outside her apartment building.
Sometimes she'd meet a neighbor
doing the same chore.

When Esther came back, she glanced
at the full-length mirror
hanging in her foyer. Just a habit.

The reflection wasn't hers.
"Oh, that's another person!" she shrieked.
And she was correct.

"I'm Hadassah," the image announced.
"I'm a golem, your golem."

"How did, why, but…" Esther stammered.
"Your yearning for a friend brought me here,"
Hadassah explained, stepping out of the mirror.
"Can I stay for a while?"

Esther craved company, but
she felt a frisson of fear go up her back.
Did she have a choice?
Crossing a golem might not be a good idea.
What should she do?

Reverting to an old habit,
Esther asked, "Would you like some coffee?"
and fled to the kitchen, putting
some space between herself and the golem.

Hadassah knew Esther was feeling anxious.
She could use her powers to calm her,
but that might make her even more afraid.
What should she do?

When Esther returned with two cups
of steaming coffee and a plate
of chocolate chip cookies,
Hadassah did what came naturally.

She smiled. And smiled again
after she sipped the drink.
And again when she took not one,
but two cookies.

Esther relaxed. She forgot this sociable
woman was a golem. Nearly forgot,
but didn't care. The two started to talk
about books and people, places
they would visit when the pandemic ended,

like two friends—now roommates.
Hadassah planned to stay until
Esther's loneliness became a mere memory.
Then she would fade away,
maybe into the mirror,
maybe to one of the alluring locales in Esther's dreams.

Golem Tastes Chocolate

Task: Find out if it's nutritious.

Luckily, Golem was created
with a mouth—a big mouth
like a sinkhole.
He ate one chocolate bar,
then a few dozen others.
Hershey's, Godiva, Mars,
made no difference to him.

Unlike a tornado,
sirens didn't warn
the nearby Russell Stover's outlet
that a mud giant
was about to strike the store.
Golem cleared out the cases
and insisted the clerk
bring him back-room stock, too.

The last thing recorded by the rabbis
was a massive tongue licking up
a pool of chocolate,
muttering, "The dark has
antioxidants."

Like Cinderella

Golem disappeared

into the night.

Shakespeare's Editor

Task: Help the Bard.

Scholars pore over an uneasy mix
of claims to authorship:
Francis Bacon, Christopher Marlowe,
Ben Jonson, Sir Walter Raleigh.
No one considers Golem
though he helped the Bard
rework several key passages.
"To be, or not to be, that is the question...."
Golem finessed Hamlet's speech
until every phrase seeded
a forest of meaning.
Just some editing. Omit a word here,
transpose a phrase there
and the speech was perfect.

"Double, double, toil and trouble;
Fire burn, and caldron bubble."
Golem told Shakespeare the witches
in *Macbeth* would be a hit
in London. He knew that in a few
centuries they would star
on Broadway and television,
in movies seen around the world.

And that play about a merchant.
Golem finessed Shylock's words
until they asked audiences
to question what they believed.
"I am a Jew. Hath not a Jew eyes?
Hath not a Jew hands, organs, dimensions,
senses, affections, passions?"

After helping the Bard with 10 plays,
Golem disappeared beneath the Globe.

The Wedding Guest

Task: Catch the bouquet.

Golem saw a *Chuppah*
of organdy and flowers
with wisps and petals
that brushed against
the wedding couple
like a kiss.
And a bridal dress whose train
flowed like warm taffy.

Wearing pink, Golem radiated
shyness so her silence seemed natural.
The bouquet, tossed toward the bride's
best friend, seemed out of reach
until Golem dipped her hands
into champagne to stretch
her mud rolls of fingers
and grab the flying stems.

When the photographer
looked for the woman
who seized the bouquet,
he found only large
and muddy pink satin shoes.
Like Cinderella,
Golem disappeared
into the night.

Ich Bin Ein Golem

Task: Destroy the Berlin Wall.

Everyone thinks Reagan was responsible.
"Mr. Gorbachev, tear down this wall."

Or the beatified Pope John Paul II
whose speeches stirred the world.

Solidarity and Lech Walesa
deserve some of the credit.

No one remembers the golem.
Who but a golem could do such a thing?

He lifted one bulging finger
with a sharp fingernail two feet long

and pressed it against the wall.
It started to teeter, then fell and everyone

jumped in to get the credit.
Crowds stumbled, then stampeded

over the concrete, now mixed with mud.
No beatification, no sainthood.

The Motorist

Task: Learn to drive.

Golem watched.
From the front passenger seat,
he memorized how his creator
shifted gears, glanced at side mirrors,
tuned to a favorite station.
How she stomped on the brake pedal
with the power of a bear
and always drove five miles over the limit.

Looked easy, but at two months old
Golem wasn't eligible for a license.
A small obstacle to mime
a sophomore in high school.
He drew in a deep breath and his body
lengthened; stubble grew on his chin;
his expression broadcast sincerity
tempered with a 16-year-old's cockiness.

Next stop the DMV and a three-hour wait
dallying with Golem's new teen psyche.
First the written test. His perfect score
as predictable as lines at Disney.
Now the driving test. Having total recall
of past road trips helped. Exceeding
the speed limit didn't. He failed.

Fortunate that his maker adored
having a chauffeur, especially one
who knew the route to every destination,
had night vision worthy of a jet pilot.

Why would she worry about a license?
If Golem were pulled over, she could
say the words that turned him back
into mud.

No one to arrest.

Wonder Golem

Task: Corroborate a child's tale.

"But the golem did it,"
the little girl explained to her mother
who scowled at her words.

"She did, she really did,"
the little girl insisted. A scissor
of anxiety cut the ends
of her words as she and her mother
examined the large hole in their yard.
Left after the golem came to life.

"Golems can't be female,"
the mother claimed.

"But they can," the child said.
"I read about golems,
and I shouted the holy words
that make them appear.
She's like *Wonder Woman,* Mom.
I didn't know what to ask her to do."

Seeing no creature anywhere
and suspecting mischief,
the woman said sarcastically,
"Order her to fill that hole
and replace the grass."

The golem rushed away,
brought back hefty divots
from a crosstown golf course
to put into the hole.

For good measure,
she transformed the entire yard
until it looked like a photo
from *Better Homes and Gardens.*
Astounded, frightened,
the woman ordered her daughter
to get rid of that creature.
As soon as possible!

Always fastidious, the golem
disappeared, leaving
a decorative frame of dirt
around the roses.

Water, Water, Nowhere

Task: Bring some drenching rain.

A golem rose when wails of thirst
flooded over creased and crumbly earth.
Around him, plants lay stunted and shredded,
air burning them like a hot iron.
Shrunken ears of corn folded into themselves
trying to hide their dun hearts.

The land needed rain
to fill streams, nourish crops,
give children puddles made for splashing.
How to get that much water?
Hydrogen. Oxygen. Easy formula
for a golem. He spent a week mixing
gases in the heavens, then steadily poured
H_2O into the cover of clouds.

The billows swelled, turned ominous colors,
astounding weather forecasters
who conjured stories worthy
of Grimm to explain the phenomenon.
When the skies held enough water
to end the drought, the golem gave
the clouds permission to release
their bounty.

Weary from his efforts,
the magical chemist rode a slide of water
down to the soil, disappeared
without leaving a footprint.

"Muddy rain," people said,
"but we'll take it."

A Golem in Wonderland

Task: Organize, organize, organize.

Saul was a collector. Of everything. When a neighbor peeked into his home, he saw a turmoil of *National Geographic* magazines, Christmas ornaments, newspapers, beer steins, hats, shoes and cuckoo clocks.

The neighbor summoned a golem to help Saul untangle his life. Crawling over piles of plastic garbage bags, the golem had a vision: "Wonderland" created from Saul's collections. He went right to work.

Clocks covered walls in heart patterns; cuckoos recited "Jabberwocky." Lawns of magazine sod stretched to hedges of unworn shirts and socks, woven to resemble spades and clubs. Ornament fountains spewed an array of Saul's tall hats. Porticos of stacked plates and teacups lined brown-bag paths.

Sitting in the kitchen, the golem was creating origami Cheshire cats, caterpillars, crowns and a hundred jesters when Saul's neighbor "galumphed" him outdoors. Then shoved him down a rabbit hole.

Words While Married

Task: Become a dictionary on demand.

Dave remembers love at first sight.
Sara's not sure, but after 45
years of marriage, she lets
Dave's memories prevail.
Their main love is each other,
main worry is Alzheimer's.
When a word sticks on Sara's tongue
and won't come out,
or a name slips under Dave's shoe
and won't come off, there's fear.

Sometimes they find
words for each other.
Together they recalled
the sacred text to conjure
a golem named Eli.

They were shocked when he appeared.
What was his purpose?
To fulfill wishes?
Dave listed things he'd buy
if he won the lottery. Sara
imagined hitting
a hole-in-one or bowling 300.
Dave rolled his eyes;
his standards were higher.

"What a smart-ass," Sara remarked,
"just like that actor in
Ferris,
  Ferris—"

"Bueller's Day Off,"
completed the golem.

Joining the conversation,
Dave added,
"Matthew,
　Matthew—"

"Broderick,"
　Eli provided.

A mission was born.
The golem helped the couple
find words and names
until the end of their days.
Then he slipped away,
leaving some dust
on their antique dictionary.

A Rose Is a Rose

Task: Acquire a new name.

The golem felt incomplete.
He knew he'd been called, "Golem,"
through the centuries
but longed for a more meaningful name,
or at least one that didn't remind him
of Tarzan's son, "Boy."
He liked Native American names
and thought of, "He Who Rises From Earth,"
but discarded that
when a local tribe threatened
to return him to earth prematurely.
Gandhi, Moses, Buddha, Maimonides,
Brad Pitt, Babe Ruth and Barack Obama were taken,
locked up tight as Crown Jewels.
He looked at names from Pakistan,
Czechoslovakia and the movie *Avatar,*
but the vowels and consonants
argued with each other like jealous siblings.
The golem listened to a fountain,
thought of, "Splash." Heard some jazz,
called himself, "Waa, Waa, Doeeee."
Eavesdropped on a man fixing a flat tire
and considered, "Damnitall,"
but discarded it when he introduced himself
to the head of the PTA.
Failing in his task, the golem was transformed
back into dirt.
A passerby found a message scratched
into mud beneath a park bench.
"My name is 'Mud' but you can call me 'Golem.'"

Deep-Fried Golem

Task: Create a new deep-fried recipe.

Golem deep fried a head of lettuce,
but discovered a Thai restaurant
served it. A delicacy,
but not an innovative dish.

Deep-fried flowers tumbled
out of her fryer next,
but cookbooks told of endless recipes
with *courgette* flowers.

Then Golem deep fried water,
tossed it into the sky
and watched it collide
with deep-fried wind.

She stared at deep-fried pollen
attracting deep-fried bees.
Tried to deep fry the sun
but forgot her sunscreen.

Finally she deep fried herself
into a cracked, gritty pie
of sand and dirt
lying under deep-fried earth.

A Golem Delivers

Task: Save a child.

Can a golem be conjured from the womb?
No, of course not.
But when Jacob was born,
a small golem appeared in his parents' yard
behind some bushes.
He looked like Jacob's twin,
same nose, eyes, wisps of hair.
Except he was still. No baby cries,
no arms waving, exploring, discovering.

As Jacob grew,
so did his golem twin, always silent.
Both reached their fifth birthdays in 1939.
Dangerous times in Prague
after *Kristallnacht* in Germany.
Rumors became real;
death loitered in corners
waiting to leap out,
clasp Jews who walked by.

Jacob's parents hid him behind a dresser
when the Nazis arrived.
As they smashed furniture,
Jacob's mother cried out.
The boy was discovered.
Destination for all,
the *Theresienstadt* ghetto,
a stop on the way to killing camps.
Outraged, the golem set a plot in motion.

All the city's Jews were rounded up,
wailing, desperate to escape.
In the chaos, the golem
blurred the air around Jacob,
rendering him invisible to the guards.
Then whispered, "Run
as fast as you can
to the red brick house
around the corner."

The golem's plan flooded
the minds of the couple
living there. When they saw
Jacob quaking on their doorstep,
they were resolved
to rescue this Jewish child,
secure him a place
on a *Kindertransport*
convoy to Britain.

Jacob's parents
were gassed. When they closed
their eyes for the last time,
they saw a vision
of their child escaping.
The final piece
of the golem's scheme.
All three rested in peace.

His mourning cries

reached deep into the earth

and created a golem.

Joining Facebook

Task: Clear up confusion.

Golem needed another name for her page.
There were countless pages already
for "G-O-L-E-M" but even more for "G-O-L-L-U-M."
Did this Sméagol think he could top her,
a golem whose ancestor saved the Jews of Prague
in the sixteenth century?
And a simple gold ring. Please.
She was magical already,
didn't need anything precious to prove it.

She visited several Facebook pages,
found Golem Taverns with hundreds
of drunken Facebook friends.
Thought of visiting a Golem Tattoo Parlor
but none of the tattoos vaguely
resembled her.
Then discovered a Golem Village in Albania.

False Gollum
attracted more than 97,000 followers.
Too frustrated to think of another name
the rabbis would approve,
Genuine Golem
bought a plane ticket and is learning Albanian.

Fallen *Shul*

Task: Save the building from demolition.

Samuel attended
the same *shul* for 50 years
and was bitter about outliving it.
Committee vote final:
Demolish. No other option.
Structure crumbling,
members moving to suburbs,
costs to repair higher
than the cantor's high C.

"It's a landmark," Samuel shouted,
"the first place Jews gathered
in this city without fear."
His mourning cries reached
deep into the earth
and created a golem.
"Help me," he pleaded
to the muscled servant
whose ancestors were known
for miracles beyond the power
of flesh and blood.

A weary voice replied.
"I am the second golem to come here.
Another defeated threats years ago
by neighbors, builders, the mayor
who tried to destroy this *shul*.

"Now, I can only deliver your message,
join my spirit with voices
etched in the collapsing stone
by thousands of repetitions.
'Hear, O Israel.'"

Attending a Funeral

Task: Offer Max a last joke.

Though not part
of his religious tradition,
a golem was taken
with the story of Lazarus.
Max's funeral offered him
the perfect opportunity
to try out his Laz skills and fulfill his task.

Bent over in a back pew,
body covered with a wool greatcoat
despite the August heat,
the golem looked like a rusted VW
as he sought to be invisible.
He concentrated
on the recently deceased, visible
in a satin-lined casket.

Obeying the golem's will,
the body started to shake.
One fist shot up,
a significant finger raised.
The miracle lasted just a few seconds.
"They don't have funerals like this anymore,"
whispered a relative who knew Max
had a bizarre sense of humor.

One mourner carried out a coat left behind.
"It's in good condition but why is it so muddy?"

Enjoying Gourmet *Matzah*

Task: Plan a perfect Seder.

An hour before *Seder*,
Gail heard a knock at her door.
"ELIJAH," she thought for a second.
But standing on her stoop was a golem
in the guise of a young girl.

"My name is Leah.
Can I join your *Seder?* I have nowhere to go."

Gail had conjured Leah
while she was practicing
the Passover story aloud.
But she didn't know it.
Leah kept the secret,
greeted Gail's other guests
as if she knew them forever.

Leah followed the *Haggadah* closely
though what intrigued her most was *matzah*.
She eagerly bit into the odd-looking square.
And choked. Then she tried another piece
shaped in an oval.
This tasted like cardboard!
Should she fix that?
Expressions around the table
answered her question.

Leah used her golem powers to add flavor
to the unleavened bread.

One woman loved chocolate.
Her husband's craving, caramel.
Gail's grandmother liked bananas.
Her uncle's addiction, raisins.
Each guest's *matzah*
now had a hint of a favorite food.

Frowns turned into smiles.
"Where did you buy this *matzah, Gail?*"
Questions were eager, excited, curious.
"Kroger," Gail replied.

Gratified, Leah changed the flavors again
for the ritual horseradish sandwich.
Essence of croissant
embraced the bitter herb.

But the *Afikomen* was Leah's tour de force.
"Find it, find it," her new friends shouted.
A no-brainer for a golem.
As Leah broke the *matzah* into pieces,
the aroma of French Vanilla
wafted into the room.

Gail's guests told her the *Seder*
was perfect, just perfect.
Then they rushed out
to search for the nearest Kroger.
Leah thanked her hostess
and disappeared into the night.
As she sank into the soil of Gail's lawn,
the melody of the Four Questions
danced down the street.

Virus vs. Golem

Task: Stop the pandemic.

Holy in its unity,
a cry from children around the globe
summoned countless golems
ready to grant their shared plea,
"Slaughter COVID-19.
Prevent it from making Mom sick,
Grandpa frightened, friends unfriendly."

Could this mystical force capture
the modern plague,
carry it back to the bats it came from?
The golems strained to stretch their skills
at magic and miracles
to destroy the infection, stop it
before it invaded another human cell.
They tried, then tried again.

Nothing worked.
The children turned away,
ordered their golems to get lost, totally lost.
The golems fought
against the command, but had to smother
their anger at failing.
Though desperate to help, they disappeared.

Later, adults noticed patches
of soil and sand that were unnaturally
discolored—blue specks, purple smudges.
Nearby ocean waves churned
as if they were boiling mad.

Golem Laughs

Task: Bring more mirth into the world.

Five minutes after rising from the earth,
Golem heard a joke
told by his creator
who couldn't help chuckling to himself
before reaching the punch line.
Golem laughed silently,
not wanting his thunderous chuckles
to drown out human laughter.
Then he felt heavy blows of quiet.
None of the other listeners
chortled, smiled or even snickered.

Feeling his maker's pain,
Golem released
laughing gas into the room.
Fumes like fingers reached out,
tickling the senses of those
who chose to sulk.
Their lips started twitching,
their eyes bulged,
their heads tilted toward the ceiling
as they hooted, guffawed and howled.
"What a sidesplitting joke!"

While the gas cleared,
Golem slipped away, leaving
a book titled *Favorite Jewish Humor*
behind.

A Golem Visits Hospice

Task: Soothe a dying woman.

Lynette was 98 years old
and alone.
Only hospice volunteers
to hold her hand until
a golem arrived.

Conjured as the nurses
discussed their patients,
the golem took the form
of Lynette's daughter
and sat at the side of her bed.

The two laughed as they shared a story
about a roast a neighbor cooked
using two garlic bulbs
instead of a couple of cloves.
There was news
about Lynette's three grandchildren,
all adults living far away,
and hand-written notes
from each one.
The golem read them aloud,
imitating their voices,
even grandson Carl's.

Before the golem's visit,
Lynette saw her past
as stale coffee, too bitter
to drink. Deaths and
disappointments had drained
flavor from her life.

Now, she felt strong when she
slipped away, a smile
on her face.
The golem joined his ashes
with hers, a gourmet blend.

Custer's Last Golem

Task: Turn the tide.

Native women tell how Mother/Father/Earth helped the Lakota, the Northern Cheyenne, the Arapaho on the day Lt. Colonel George Armstrong Custer hoped to slaughter their warriors and take families hostage. None of the people saw a golem standing by the Little Bighorn River, studying Custer and his 210 men. Blankets of tree and brush kept Custer from gauging the size of the village he hunted, a village much larger than he assumed. Custer didn't trust his native scouts' warnings. Merely women and children, he thought. Easy prey.

The golem watched until the battle began. Then he transformed his body into a large knoll, luring the soldiers to hide behind him, fire guns there, feel safe. The golem knew arrows, aimed at puffs of smoke rising from the soldiers' weapons, would fly above the knoll, then plummet like stampeding buffalo, killing clusters of troops.

Did that make a difference? To this day, the exact reason why Custer lost the Battle of Little Bighorn is still debated. A golem is never part of the argument for either side.

Buried in the battlefield are Custer and his regiment. Buried at its edge is the golem, refusing to blend his remains with leaders of the American Holocaust.

Dishing on Liz

Task: Discover the true color of her eyes.

Liz Taylor had passed on
but that didn't stop a golem from his search.
He convinced the rabbis to allow him to visit
the afterlife. (Ever since her conversion,
they were obsessed with her.)
The golem inhaled her perfumes
as soon as he passed through
the big gold-plated gates.
It took him only five minutes
to reach a table of Jewish women
playing Mah-Jongg, their ears splashed
with Liz's signature scents.
Passion, White Diamonds, Black Pearls.
The group readily gave him directions.
There she was, sitting by a pool
with Conrad, Mike W, Mike T,
Eddie, John, Larry and Rich times two.

All those luminaries together.
A jungle of vines
encircling a single exotic flower.
The golem doubted Liz would let him come near
since he had the features of a dirt ball.
So he gathered mounds of cigarette butts,
fused a few into rows for his eyebrows,
sliced lipstick-stained ends for lips,
feathered tobacco for lashes.
Then the golem grabbed a tray of martinis,
his offering to the queen Liz was.

Who would have guessed that this nice
Jewish girl would know the sacred words
that would turn the golem back into dust?

His last thought—periwinkle.

Impossible Dilemma

Task: Shoot without mercy.

The legends convey a clear message:
Evil people can't summon a golem.
But survivors say it happened.
In Budapest
during the '56 Hungarian revolution.
Hiding behind protesting men and women,
a vile man conjured a golem,
handed him a rifle and ordered him to shoot
Hungarian soldiers, Soviet soldiers,
children huddled in doorways,
students waving signs flashy as lightning.

Create total chaos.

Perplexed, the golem begged
his creator to let him
transform into a slavering monster
shrieking like a nightmare
to scatter his targets, not kill them.
But the man wouldn't allow
any deviation.
"My command is carved
into the earth of your being," he said.
"You have no choice."

The golem looked into the souls
within the range of his weapon,
saw a microcosm of mankind,
mixed rations of noble, wicked
and everything in between.

With clear understanding,
the golem knew what he had to do.
Yes, he would use the rifle
placed in his hands,
blast himself
back into fragments of earth,
reclaim his destiny
of dust to dust.

Momentous Belch

Task: Control crowds.

When it came to epic belching,
Golem's Jewish heritage
gave him the ingredients he needed:
gastric grenades of corned beef, pastrami,
pickles, cabbage soup, gefilte fish, lox.
Lethal, especially mixed with whiffs of mud.

Golem called it, "The Belch Solution"
and advertised he could emit golem-sized
bursts of gas to clear out crowded elevators,
send tall guys fleeing to back rows,
shorten lines at Disneyland.
Simply text GOBELCH and he'd reach you
with the speed of a bullet train.

But Golem's days as an entrepreneur
ended abruptly when a ten-year-old
decided to use his services to skip *Cheder.*
The kid's teacher turned Golem's performance
into a lesson. Had the entire class
repeat the Hebrew words that,
like a Divine antacid,
ended Golem's career.

Glossary

On the March
Yarmulke: Skullcap.

Escape Now
Kristallnacht: A pogrom in 1938 against Jews in Nazi Germany known as "The Night of Broken Glass."

The Wedding Guest
Chuppah: Marriage Canopy.

Deep-Fried Golem
Courgette: Zucchini.

A Golem Delivers
Kindertransport: Mission that saved thousands of Jewish children by taking them by train from Nazi-occupied Europe to the United Kingdom and other countries.

Fallen *Shul*
Shul: Synagogue.

Enjoying Gourmet *Matzah*
Seder: Ritual Passover meal.
Haggadah: Guide recited at the *Seder*.
Matzah: Unleavened flatbread.
Horseradish sandwich: Called the Hillel Sandwich. The horseradish represents bitter herbs that symbolize the bitterness of slavery.
Afikomen: A piece of *matzah* set aside or hidden early in the *Seder* to be found by children or the youngest person attending. It is then broken into pieces and eaten as a dessert.
Four Questions: Text sung during the *Seder* by the youngest person at the table.

Momentous Belch
Cheder: Hebrew School.

About the Author

Tina Hacker was a sophomore at the University of Illinois when a woman in her dormitory slipped an unfriendly note under her door. Shocked, she shed a few tears and wrote her first poem. Then, with encouragement from teachers and friends, she spent every spare minute writing poems. Within a year, her work was accepted by journals from the Universities of Wisconsin and Illinois.

Today, Tina lives in Leawood, KS, with her husband Lynn Norton and is an active member of the area's literary community. She served as Co-president of The Writers Place in Kansas City, MO, and Vice-president of the eight-state Midwest Region for Women in Communications. She is the recipient of the Matrix Honor Prize in Communications and, in 2016, was named a Muse of The Writers Place. Since 1976, Tina has been poetry editor for *Veterans' Voices,* a national magazine of prose, poetry, and art by military veterans.

A four-time Pushcart Prize nominee, Tina was a finalist in *New Letters* and George F. Wedge contests. She was Editor's Choice in two journals and has been published in numerous anthologies and journals such as the *San Pedro River Review, Glass: A Journal of Poetry, The Fib Review, The Whirlybird Anthology of Kansas City Writers, The Ekphrastic Review,* and *I-70 Review.*

Tina's chapbook, *Cutting It,* was published by The Lives You Touch Publications. She is also the author of *Listening to Night Whistles,* published by Aldrich Press and available on Amazon.

www.ingramcontent.com/pod-product-compliance
Lightning Source LLC
Chambersburg PA
CBHW071357090426

42738CB00012B/3145